LITERATURE
WORKS

An Integrated Approach to
Reading and Language Arts

D1541385

READING AND LANGUAGE ARTS SKILLS ASSESSMENT TEACHER'S MANUAL

GRADE 1 / 3

SILVER BURDETT GINN

Needham, MA   Parsippany, NJ

Atlanta, GA   Deerfield, IL   Irving, TX   Santa Clara, CA

Silver Burdett Ginn
A Division of Simon & Schuster
160 Gould Street
Needham Heights, MA 02194

ISBN: 0-663-59599-1   3 4 5 6 7 8 9 10 CO 01 00 99 98 97 96

Collection 1

Using This Manual

This manual contains the directions for administering and scoring the Reading and Language Arts Skills Assessment for Collection 1, Book 3 in *Literature Works*. Grade 1 has eight themes and three separate Skills Assessment Manuals. The tests described in this manual are designed to assess children's understanding of the tested skills taught in Themes 5 and 6. The chart on pages T3–4 identifies all skills tested in Grade 1 and the points at which they are tested.

The individual test for each theme contains three or four subtests: vocabulary, comprehension, phonics, and, in Theme 5, study skills. Each subtest begins with a sample.

Helping Children Feel at Ease

People generally perform better when they feel at ease in a situation. These tests are designed to match the instruction children have received in *Literature Works*. The questions are similar in format to those children have seen. Thus, children should feel at ease with the format and content of the tests.

Another part of feeling at ease in a situation is knowing what to expect. Each section of the test begins with a sample of the material in that section. Working through the sample with the class helps children know what to expect and provides an opportunity for them to ask questions before they proceed.

The testing environment should be one that is comfortable. It should be reasonably quiet and free of interruptions.

Making Testing a Positive Experience

Since these tests parallel instruction, children who have profited from instruction should do well on them.

These tests may be administered in more flexible ways than standardized tests. There are no time limits, nor is it necessary to administer the test in a single sitting.

Test administration may be adapted to the needs of your class. Guidelines for administering the tests and discussing the samples are given in this manual. If there is specific wording that you think will help children understand the tests better, use such language with your class.

Scheduling the Test

The test should be administered when children have completed the corresponding theme or themes in *Literature Works*. Although there is no time limit, each testing session should not last too long. Before giving the test, look over the questions and estimate how much time children will need. You may choose to give the complete test at one time, or you may want to break the testing into two or more sessions.

Materials Needed

Each child will need a copy of the appropriate Skills Assessment booklet, a few sharp pencils, and an eraser.

You will need to use this manual to administer the tests. You may find it helpful to have an extra test booklet that you can hold up to show children what page they should turn to.

Directions for scoring the test are also contained in this manual. Scores can be recorded on the Student Record Form (found in the Student's Test Booklet), the Class Profile (found in the back of this manual), and the Student Progress Card (available separately).

General Orientation for Children

Before you hand out test materials, you may wish to give children an overview of the test. Tell them that they will be taking a test based on the *Literature Works* theme or themes they have just completed. Explain that the test will be like the work they've been doing in class.

Tell children that each section of the test begins with a sample of the kind of questions in that section. Explain that you will be doing the samples together. Children may find it helpful if you copy and complete each sample item on the chalkboard as they do the one in their test booklet. Encourage children to ask questions about the sample so that you can be sure each child understands what to do.

STRAND	Skill	Theme
VOCABULARY	Tested Vocabulary	1–2, 3–4, Mid-Year, 5, 6, 7, 8, End-of-Year
COMPREHENSION	Cause and Effect	6, End-of-Year
	Classify and Categorize	1–2, Mid-Year
	Compare and Contrast	5, 8
	Drawing Conclusions	6, 8
	Reality and Fantasy	5, End-of-Year
	Main Idea and Details	3–4, Mid-Year, 8
	Predicting Outcomes	1–2, Mid-Year, 8
	Sequence	7, 8
	Character Traits/ Characterization	7, End-of-Year
	Note Details	3–4, Mid-Year
PHONICS	Initial Consonants	1–2, 3–4, Mid-Year
	Final Consonants	1–2, 3–4, Mid-Year
	Digraphs	3–4, 6
	Phonograms	3–4, Mid-Year, 5
	Consonant Blends	3–4, 5, End-of-Year
	Short Vowels	6, 7, 8, End-of-Year
	Long Vowels	6, 8, End-of-Year

continued

STRAND	Skill	Theme
STUDY SKILLS	ABC Order	5, 7
	Following Directions	7, End-of-Year

Vocabulary

After handing out test booklets, tell children to turn to the sample items on page 1. If you like, write the sample items on the chalkboard. Say aloud:

> Open your booklets to page 1. Find the box with the star and heart in it. These are samples for us to use for practice. We are going to do these together.

Check to see that children are looking at the sample items.

> Look at the sentence next to the star. Read the sentence to yourself while I read it aloud. There is a word missing from the sentence. I will pause where the word is missing. Listen. *The book is* (pause).

> Now look at the three words below the sentence. Read them to yourself while I read them aloud: *city, mine, all*. Which word best completes the sentence, *The book is* (pause)?

Ask a child to give the answer.

> Yes, the word *mine* best completes the sentence, *The book is mine*. Now look at the answer circle in front of the word *mine*. What letter is in the circle?

Ask a child to give the answer.

> Yes, the letter *B* is in the answer circle in front of the word *mine*. Fill in answer circle *B* with your pencil.

If necessary, fill in the answer circle on the chalkboard. Check to see that children have filled in the correct answer circle.

> Are there any questions?

Follow the same procedure for the second sentence in the sample. The correct answer for the second item is C.

Make sure that children understand what they are to do.

Then read aloud with children the remaining sentences, items 1 through 10, and the word choices. Have children answer each item independently by filling in the circle in front of what they think is the best answer. Alternatively, if children are able to do so, you might have them read the sentences and complete the items independently.

Comprehension:
Reality/Fantasy,
Compare/Contrast

Tell the children to turn to the sample story on page 4. Say aloud:

> Now look at the story in the box with the star. This is a sample for us to use for practice. We are going to do this one together.

Check to see that children are looking at the sample item.

> Now look at the picture of the animals on the farm. We will read a story about them. Then we will answer some questions about the story.

Read the story aloud with children.

> Now look at the top of the next page. We will read the first question next to the star together. *What could* not happen *in real life?* Now we'll read the answer choices below the question: *The farmer drove his truck, The cow painted the barn, The farmer worked hard on the farm.*

> Which one is the best answer?

Ask a child to give the answer and to explain his or her choice.

> Yes, the best answer is *The cow painted the barn*. The farmer can drive a truck and work hard but a cow cannot paint a barn. What letter is in the answer circle in front of the sentence *The cow painted the barn*?

Ask a child to give the answer.

> Yes, the letter *B* is in the answer circle in front of the sentence *The cow painted the barn*. Fill in answer circle *B* with your pencil.

Check to see that children have filled in the correct answer circle. Guide children through the second sample question in the same way. The correct answer to the second question is C.

Are there any questions?

Make sure children understand what they are to do.

Then read aloud with children the remaining passages, items 11 through 18, and the answer choices. Have children answer each item independently by filling in the circle in front of what they think is the best answer. Alternatively, if children are able to do so, you might have them read the sentences and complete the items independently.

Phonics:
Phonograms

PLEASE NOTE: We strongly recommend that you read aloud the picture name for each item in this subtest.

Tell children to turn to page 12. If you like, write the sample item on the chalkboard. Say aloud:

Find the box with the star in it. This is a sample for us to use for practice. We are going to do this one together.

Check to see that children are looking at the sample item.

Look at the picture of the dish next to the star. Look at the three words beside the picture of the dish. Put your finger on the word *dish*. What letter is in the answer circle in front of the word *dish*?

Ask a child to give the answer.

Yes, the letter *B* is in the answer circle in front of the word *dish*. Fill in answer circle *B* with your pencil.

If necessary, fill in the answer circle on the chalkboard. Check to see that children have filled in the correct answer circle.

Are there any questions?

Make sure children understand what they are to do.
Item 19, page 12:

Now look at the first row under the box. Find the picture of the pig. Now look at the three words beside the picture. Fill in the answer circle in front of the word *pig*.

Continue in the same way for items 20 through 22. Say each picture name aloud so all children look for the same word. Alternatively, if children are able to do so, you might have them read the words and complete the items independently.

20. swim   21. ten   22. kick

Phonics:
Consonant blends

PLEASE NOTE: We strongly recommend that you read aloud the picture name for each item in this subtest.

Tell children to turn to page 13. If you like, write the sample item on the chalkboard. Say aloud:

Find the box with the star in it. This is a sample for us to use for practice. We are going to do this one together.

Check to see that children are looking at the sample item.

Look at the picture of the glass. Look at the three pairs of letters beside the picture of the glass. Which letters stand for the sounds you hear at the beginning of the word *glass*? Put your finger on the letters *gl*. What letter is in the answer circle in front of the letters *gl*?

Ask a child to give the answer.

Yes, the letter *C* is in the answer circle in front of the letters *gl*. Fill in answer circle *C* with your pencil.

If necessary, fill in the answer circle on the chalkboard. Check to see that children have filled in the correct answer circle.

Are there any questions?

Make sure children understand what they are to do.
Item 23, page 13:

Now look at the first row under the box. Find the picture of the slide. Now look at the three pairs of letters beside the picture. Fill in the answer circle in front of the letters that stand for the sounds you hear at the beginning of the word *slide*.

Continue in the same way for items 24 through 26. Say each picture name aloud so all children look for the same pairs of letters. Alternatively, if children are able to do so, you might have them read the words and complete the items independently.

24. flag   25. clown   26. plant

Study Skills:
ABC order

Tell children to turn to page 14. If you like, write the sample item on the chalkboard. Say aloud:

Find the box with the star in it. This is a sample for us to use for practice together.

Check to see that the children are looking at the sample item.

Look at the words next to the star. We will read the words together: <u>f</u>og, <u>r</u>abbit, <u>c</u>at. The first letter of each word is underlined. Look at the letters *f*, *r*, and *c*. Which letter comes first in ABC order?

Ask a child to give the answer.

Yes, the letter *c* comes first. What word comes first in ABC order?

Ask a child to give the answer.

Yes, the word *cat* comes first in ABC order. Now look at the letter in the circle in front of the word *cat*. What letter is in the circle?

Ask a child to give the answer.

Yes, the letter *C* is in the answer box in front of the word *cat*. Fill in the answer circle *C* with your pencil.

If necessary fill in the answer circle on the chalkboard. Check to see that the children have filled in the correct answer circle.

Are there any questions?

Make sure the children understand what they are to do.

Continue in the same way for items 27 through 30. Read each word aloud. Tell children they can underline the first letter of each word, if they wish. Alternatively, if children are able to do so, you might have them read the words and complete the items independently.

27. read   give   see

28. note   table   room

29. sing   fed   pay

30. cows   lions   bears

Vocabulary

After handing out test booklets, tell children to turn to the sample items on page 16. If you like, write the sample items on the chalkboard. Say aloud:

> **Open your booklets to page 16. Find the box with the star and heart in it. These are samples for us to use for practice. We are going to do these together.**

Check to see that children are looking at the sample items.

> **Look at the sentence next to the star. Read the sentence to yourself while I read it aloud. There is a word missing from the sentence. I will pause where the word is missing. Listen.** *It's time for* **(pause).**

> **Now look at the three words below the sentence. Read them to yourself while I read them aloud:** *sky, breakfast, down.* **Which word best completes the sentence,** *It's time for* **(pause)?**

Ask a child to give the answer.

> **Yes, the word** *breakfast* **best completes the sentence,** *It's time for breakfast.* **Now look at the answer circle in front of the word** *breakfast.* **What letter is in the circle?**

> **Yes, the letter** *B* **is in the answer circle in front of the word** *breakfast.* **Fill in answer circle** *B* **with your pencil.**

If necessary, fill in the answer circle on the chalkboard. Check to see that children have filled in the correct answer circle.

> **Are there any questions?**

Follow the same procedure for the second sentence in the sample. The correct answer for the second item is C.

Make sure that children understand what they are to do.

Then read aloud with children the remaining sentences, items 1 through 10, and the word choices. Have children answer each item independently by filling in the circle in front of what they think is the best answer. Alternatively, if children are able to do so, you might have them read the passages and complete the items independently.

Comprehension:
Cause and Effect,
Drawing conclusions

Tell the children to turn to the sample story on page 18. Say aloud:

> **Now look at the story in the box with the star. This is a sample for us to use for practice. We are going to do this one together.**

Check to see that children are looking at the sample item.

> **Now look at the picture of the girl reading her book. We will read a story about her. Then we will answer some questions about the story.**

Read the story aloud with children.

> **Now look at the top of the next page. We will read the beginning of the sentence next to the star together.** *Maria was happy because* ___. **Now we'll read the answer choices below the beginning of the sentence:** *summer had come, she lived in a cold place, her mother could swim.* **Which one is the best answer?**

Ask a child to give the answer and to explain his or her choice.

> **Yes, the best answer is** *summer had come.* **The story said that summer was Maria's favorite time. What letter is in the answer circle in front of the sentence** *summer had come?*

Ask a child to give the answer.

> **Yes, the letter** *A* **is in the answer circle in front of the sentence** *summer had come.* **Fill in answer circle** *A* **with your pencil.**

Check to see that children have filled in the correct answer circle. Guide children through the second sample question in the same way. The correct answer to the second question is B.

Are there any questions?

Make sure children understand what they are to do.

Then read aloud with children the remaining passages, items 11 through 18, and the answer choices. Have children answer each item independently by filling in the circle in front of what they think is the best answer. Alternatively, if children are able to do so, you might have them read the passages and complete the items independently.

Phonics:
Short vowels

PLEASE NOTE: We strongly recommend that you read aloud the picture name for each item in this subtest.

Tell children to turn to page 24. If you like, write the sample item on the chalkboard. Say aloud:

Find the box with the star in it. This is a sample for us to use for practice. We are going to do this one together.

Check to see that children are looking at the sample item.

Look at the picture of the bat. Look at the three words beside the picture of the bat. Put your finger on the word *bat*. What letter is in the answer circle in front of the word *bat*?

Ask a child to give the answer.

Yes, the letter *B* is in the answer circle in front of the word *bat*. Fill in answer circle *B* with your pencil.

If necessary, fill in the answer circle on the chalkboard. Check to see that children have filled in the correct answer circle.

Are there any questions?

Make sure children understand what they are to do.

Item 19, page 24:

Now look at the first row under the box. Find the picture of the *pin*. Now look at the three words beside the picture. Fill in the answer circle in front of the word *pin*.

Continue in the same way for items 20 through 22. Say each picture name aloud so all children look for the same word. Alternatively, if children are able to do so, you might have them read the words and complete the items independently.

20. net   21. mop   22. rip

Phonics:
Long vowels

PLEASE NOTE: We strongly recommend that you read aloud the picture name for each item in this subtest.

Tell children to turn to page 25. If you like, write the sample item on the chalkboard. Say aloud:

Find the box with the star in it. This is a sample for us to use for practice. We are going to do this one together.

Check to see that children are looking at the sample item.

Look at the picture of the bike. Look at the three words beside the picture of the bike. Put your finger on the word *bike*. What letter is in the answer circle in front of the word *bike*?

Ask a child to give the answer.

Yes, the letter *B* is in the answer circle in front of the word *bike*. Fill in answer circle *B* with your pencil.

Reading and Language Arts Skills Assessment

COLLECTION 1/3

SILVER BURDETT GINN

Silver Burdett Ginn
A Division of Simon & Schuster
160 Gould Street
Needham Heights, MA 02194

1997 Printing.
© 1996 Silver Burdett Ginn Inc.

ISBN: 0-663-59589-4   3 4 5 6 7 8 9 10 CO 01 00 99 98 97 96

ACKNOWLEDGMENTS

COVER: *Design:* Dinardo Design; *Illustration:* Ashley Van Etten.

Name _____

Samples

★ The book is _____.

   Ⓐ city   Ⓑ mine   Ⓒ all

♥ I _____ at the book.

   Ⓐ our   Ⓑ tall   Ⓒ looked

---

1. We were singing and _____.

   Ⓐ make   Ⓑ dancing   Ⓒ ducks

2. Do you know _____ is in the box?

   Ⓐ then   Ⓑ looked   Ⓒ what

3. The cat got up and _____ away.

   Ⓐ walked   Ⓑ sound   Ⓒ bird

4. I picked a red _____.

   Ⓐ flower   Ⓑ little   Ⓒ eating

GO

Name _____

5. Bill sat at the _____.

    Ⓐ squirrel   Ⓑ what   Ⓒ table

6. Mary is playing in her _____.

    Ⓐ room   Ⓑ lions   Ⓒ note

7. We saw the ducks _____ over the lake.

    Ⓐ mine   Ⓑ fly   Ⓒ tree

8. The rain helps to _____ the street.

    Ⓐ clean   Ⓑ soon   Ⓒ room

9. Look at that big _____ in the sky.

    Ⓐ walked   Ⓑ city   Ⓒ cloud

10. We went to sleep _____ we ate.

    Ⓐ under   Ⓑ after   Ⓒ from

Sample

★ A Day at the Farm

Farmer Ben worked hard on his farm. One day he had to go to town. He said to the animals, "I need your help. You must take care of the farm while I am away."

So Farmer Ben went away in his truck. The animals began to work.

Gus Goat took wood to the barn. Penny Pig fed the little ducks. Hal Horse worked in the garden. Kelly Cow painted the barn. The animals were happy working together.

When Farmer Ben got back, he looked around his farm. He said, "You all did a good job. Thank you."

Samples

★ What could <u>not</u> <u>happen</u> in real life?

　Ⓐ The farmer drove his truck.

　Ⓑ The cow painted the barn.

　Ⓒ The farmer worked hard on the farm.

♥ How were Farmer Ben's animals alike?

　Ⓐ They all painted the barn.

　Ⓑ They all worked in the garden.

　Ⓒ They all liked to work on the farm.

Sleepy Sal

Sal was sleeping. "Wake up!" said his father. "It's time to get out of bed." Sal pulled the covers over his head. "Wake up!" said Sal's mother. "It's time to get up."

"Get up!" said Sal's cat. "Get out of bed and eat your breakfast." Sal's dog pulled the covers off the bed.

Sal opened his eyes and got out of bed. He ate his breakfast. "It is Saturday!" he said. "I can play or ride my bike.

"Come and play with me," he said to the cat and the dog. But they did not move. They were sleeping.

Name _____

11. What <u>could</u> <u>not</u> happen in real life?

 Ⓐ Sal liked to sleep.

 Ⓑ The cat talked to Sal.

 Ⓒ Sal ate breakfast.

12. How were Sal's mother and father alike?

 Ⓐ They were both sleeping.

 Ⓑ They were both feeding the cat.

 Ⓒ They both wanted Sal to wake up.

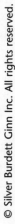

GO

Let's Swim

One day, Fred Frog wanted to go for a swim.

Fred Frog looked for a friend to swim with him. First he asked Kit Cat. "Come swim with me in the pond," he said.

Kit Cat did not like water. She said, "No, a pond is no place for a cat."

Next, Fred Frog said to Blue Bird, "Come swim with me in the pond."

But Blue Bird did not like the water. She said, "No, a pond is no place for a bird."

Fred Frog was sad. He had no friend to swim with him. Then, he saw Tom Turtle. Fred said, "Come swim with me in the pond."

"Yes," said Tom Turtle. "The pond is a good place for a turtle."

Name _____

13. What could <u>not</u> <u>happen</u> in real life?

    Ⓐ A frog and a turtle swim in a pond.

    Ⓑ A frog talks to a cat.

    Ⓒ A bird sits in her nest.

14. How are Fred Frog and Tom Turtle alike?

    Ⓐ They both wanted to swim.

    Ⓑ They both have a shell.

    Ⓒ They both can hop.

15. How are Blue Bird and Kit Cat alike?

    Ⓐ They both can fly.

    Ⓑ They both have four feet.

    Ⓒ They both don't like to swim.

The Race

Lamar got a new bike for his birthday. He wanted to race with his dog, Red.

"I will race you to the park," Lamar said to Red. "I can go fast on my bike."

"I can run faster because I have four legs. I will win the race," said Red.

They both went very fast. Lamar got to the park first. "I win," said Lamar. Red wanted to race again. He asked Lamar to race back to the house.

They raced again. This time Red was first. "I win this time," said Red.

"That was a good race," said Lamar. "Yes, I like to race," said Red.

Name _____

16. What <u>could</u> <u>not</u> happen in real life?

    Ⓐ A dog runs fast.

    Ⓑ A boy rides a bike.

    Ⓒ A dog asks Lamar to race.

17. How are Lamar and his dog alike?

    Ⓐ They both have a tail.

    Ⓑ They both like to race.

    Ⓒ They both read books.

18. What <u>could</u> happen in real life?

    Ⓐ Red asked Lamar to race.

    Ⓑ Lamar rode his bike very fast.

    Ⓒ The dog could count.

Name _____

19.   Ⓐ pick   Ⓑ pen   Ⓒ pig

20.  Ⓐ swim   Ⓑ sick   Ⓒ swish

21.   Ⓐ tick   Ⓑ tap   Ⓒ ten

22.   Ⓐ kin   Ⓑ kick   Ⓒ kite

Name _____

		Sample		
★		Ⓐ gr	Ⓑ pl	Ⓒ gl

23.   Ⓐ sl   Ⓑ gl   Ⓒ sp

24.   Ⓐ pl   Ⓑ fl   Ⓒ fr

25.   Ⓐ cr   Ⓑ pl   Ⓒ cl

26.   Ⓐ pl   Ⓑ pr   Ⓒ sl

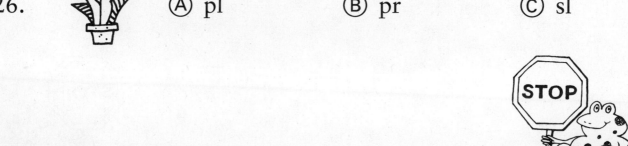

Name _____

27.   Ⓐ read   Ⓑ give   Ⓒ see

28.   Ⓐ note   Ⓑ table   Ⓒ room

29.   Ⓐ sing   Ⓑ fed   Ⓒ pay

30.   Ⓐ cows   Ⓑ lions   Ⓒ bears

Student Name _____ Test Date _____

STRAND/Skill/Items	Student **Skill** Score	Suggested Passing Score	Student **Strand** Score	Suggested Passing Score
VOCABULARY				
tested vocabulary				
1 _____ 2 _____ 3 _____ 4 _____ 5 _____				
6 _____ 7 _____ 8 _____ 9 _____ 10 _____	_____	8/10	_____	8/10
COMPREHENSION				
compare and contrast				
12 _____ 14 _____ 15 _____ 17 _____	_____	3/4		
reality and fantasy				
11 _____ 13 _____ 16 _____ 18 _____	_____	3/4	_____	6/8
PHONICS				
phonograms				
19 _____ 20 _____ 21 _____ 22 _____	_____	3/4		
consonant blends				
23 _____ 24 _____ 25 _____ 26 _____	_____	3/4	_____	6/8
STUDY SKILLS				
abc order				
27 _____ 28 _____ 29 _____ 30 _____	_____	3/4	_____	3/4
Total Test Score:			_____	23/30

Recommendations: _____

_____

_____

_____

_____

Teacher _____ Grade _____ School _____

Name _____

Samples

 It's time for ____.

  Ⓐ sky　　　　Ⓑ breakfast　　　Ⓒ down

 I'll ____ you my new book.

  Ⓐ or　　　　Ⓑ sun　　　　　Ⓒ show

---

1. Do you know what ____ it is?

  Ⓐ time　　　　Ⓑ best　　　　Ⓒ took

2. I know how ____ I am.

  Ⓐ old　　　　Ⓑ book　　　　Ⓒ note

3. When I got in the house, I took my hat ____.

  Ⓐ when　　　　Ⓑ today　　　　Ⓒ off

4. When it rained, I got ____.

  Ⓐ first　　　　Ⓑ wet　　　　Ⓒ were

Name _____

5. I walked _____ the hill.

   Ⓐ way   Ⓑ rain   Ⓒ down

6. I go to sleep at _____.

   Ⓐ night   Ⓑ wind   Ⓒ money

7. We got to the show just after it _____.

   Ⓐ won't   Ⓑ began   Ⓒ best

8. When we go home, we say _____.

   Ⓐ wasn't   Ⓑ good-bye   Ⓒ around

9. After school, my father _____ me home.

   Ⓐ better   Ⓑ could   Ⓒ took

10. I lost my ball _____ in the park.

   Ⓐ wind   Ⓑ sun   Ⓒ somewhere

STOP

★ What To Do?

Maria was very happy. School was out for the summer. Summer was her favorite time. Now she could play all day. She liked to swim and ride her bike. She liked to play ball. She liked to sit under a tree and read a book. She liked to play with her friends in the park.

There were so many things to do. Maria didn't know what she wanted to do first.

Samples

★ Maria was happy because _____.

   Ⓐ summer had come

   Ⓑ she lived in a cold place

   Ⓒ her mother could swim

♥ Maria could play outside all day because _____.

   Ⓐ she found her book

   Ⓑ school was out

   Ⓒ it was raining

Too Hot

It was a warm summer day and Tim was hot. He drank some water. He was still very hot. He ate ice cream, but he was still hot.

Tim sat under the tree with his book. He was still hot. "I can't cool down!" said Tim. Tim saw Lee walking with her friends. They were walking to Lee's house. "I'm so hot," said Tim. "How can I get cool?"

"Come with us, Tim," said Lee. We are going to use the hose to get cool.

Tim put down his book and went with Lee and her friends. They all went to Lee's house. She turned on the hose and let her friends run through the water.

After Tim ran through the water from the hose, he said, "I feel much better."

Name _____

11. Tim was hot because ____.

   Ⓐ the water was warm

   Ⓑ it was a warm day

   Ⓒ he was hungry

12. Lee said "Come with us" because she wanted to ____.

   Ⓐ be helpful

   Ⓑ read Tim's book

   Ⓒ go home

13. Tim sat under the tree because ____.

   Ⓐ he was waiting for a friend

   Ⓑ he forgot to have supper

   Ⓒ he wanted to feel cool

14. After he went to Lee's house, Tim felt better

   because ____.

   Ⓐ he had friends to play with

   Ⓑ he read a book

   Ⓒ he ran through the water from the hose

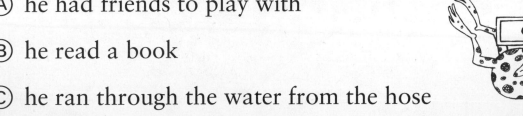

The Storm

  Rosa was looking out the window. She saw a dark cloud move across the sky. It covered the sun. Rosa knew a storm was coming. She knew she could not go out to play.

  The wind started to blow. Trees were bending and leaves flew through the air. The door closed with a loud bang! The birds knew the storm was coming. They hid under the porch roof to get away.

  The rain started to fall. First came a soft pit-pat. Then the sound got louder and louder. It sounded like a drummer beating on the roof.

Name _____

15. Rosa did not go outside because _____.

Ⓐ she wanted to read

Ⓑ a storm was coming

Ⓒ she saw the birds

16. Where will Rosa play when the storm comes?

Ⓐ in her yard   Ⓑ in her house   Ⓒ in the park

17. Why did the birds go under the porch roof?

Ⓐ to find food

Ⓑ to play with a cat

Ⓒ to get away from the storm

18. The door closed with a bang because _____.

Ⓐ the wind blew it shut

Ⓑ the birds banged into it

Ⓒ Rosa pushed it

Name _____

Sample

 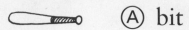 Ⓐ bit   Ⓑ bat   Ⓒ bet

19.   Ⓐ pin   Ⓑ pan   Ⓒ pen

20.   Ⓐ not   Ⓑ net   Ⓒ note

21.   Ⓐ mope   Ⓑ mop   Ⓒ map

22.   Ⓐ ripe   Ⓑ rap   Ⓒ rip

Name _____

Sample

★   Ⓐ bake   Ⓑ bike   Ⓒ back

23.   Ⓐ cane   Ⓑ cone   Ⓒ can

24.   Ⓐ bit   Ⓑ bee   Ⓒ bed

25.   Ⓐ dad   Ⓑ dim   Ⓒ dime

26.   Ⓐ bone   Ⓑ band   Ⓒ bin

Name _____

Sample

  Ⓐ th   Ⓑ sh   Ⓒ ch

27.  Ⓐ wh   Ⓑ th   Ⓒ sh

28.   Ⓐ ch   Ⓑ sh   Ⓒ wh

29.  Ⓐ sh   Ⓑ ch   Ⓒ th

30.   Ⓐ th   Ⓑ wh   Ⓒ ch

Student Name _____ Test Date _____

STRAND/Skill/Items	Student **Skill** Score	Suggested Passing Score	Student **Strand** Score	Suggested Passing Score
VOCABULARY				
tested vocabulary				
1 ____ 2 ____ 3 ____ 4 ____ 5 ____				
6 ____ 7 ____ 8 ____ 9 ____ 10 ____	____	8/10	____	8/10
COMPREHENSION				
cause and effect				
11 ____ 13 ____ 15 ____ 18 ____	____	3/4		
drawing conclusions				
12 ____ 14 ____ 16 ____ 17 ____	____	3/4	____	6/8
PHONICS				
short vowels				
19 ____ 20 ____ 21 ____ 22 ____	____	3/4		
long vowels				
23 ____ 24 ____ 25 ____ 26 ____	____	3/4		
digraphs				
27 ____ 28 ____ 29 ____ 30 ____	____	3/4	____	9/12
Total Test Score:			____	23/30

Recommendations: _____

_____

_____

_____

Teacher _____ Grade _____ School _____

LITERATURE
WORKS

ISBN 0-663-59589-4

00001

SILVER BURDETT GINN

If necessary, fill in the answer circle on the chalkboard. Check to see that children have filled in the correct answer circle.

Are there any questions?

Make sure children understand what they are to do.
Item 23, page 25:

Now look at the first row under the box. Find the picture of the cane. Now look at the three words beside the picture. Fill in the answer circle in front of the word *cane*.

Continue in the same way for items 24 through 26. Say each picture name aloud so all children look for the same letter. Alternatively, if children are able to do so, you might have them read the words and complete the items independently.

24. bee   25. dime   26. bone

Phonics:
Digraphs

PLEASE NOTE: We strongly recommend that you read aloud the picture name for each item in this subtest.

Tell children to turn to page 26. If you like, write the sample item on the chalkboard. Say aloud:

Find the box with the star in it. This is a sample for us to use for practice. We are going to do this one together.

Check to see that children are looking at the sample item.

Look at the picture of the chair. Look at the three pairs of letters beside the picture of the chair. Which letters stand for the sound you hear at the beginning of the word *chair*? Put your finger on the letters *ch*. What letter is in the answer circle in front of the letter *ch*?

Ask a child to give the answer.

Yes, the letter C is in the answer circle in front of the letters *ch*. Fill in answer circle C with your pencil.

If necessary, fill in the answer circle on the chalkboard. Check to see that children have filled in the correct answer circle.

Are there any questions?

Make sure children understand what they are to do.
Item 27, page 26:

Now look at the first row under the box. Find the picture of the thumb. Now look at the three pairs of letters beside the picture. Fill in the answer circle in front of the letters that stand for the sound you hear at the beginning of the word *thumb*.

Continue in the same way for items 28 through 30. Say each picture name aloud so all children look for the same letter. Alternatively, if children are able to do so, you might have them read the words and complete the items independently.

28. whistle   29. shoe   30. chest

Scoring and Recording Test Results

Two forms, the Student Record Form and the Class Profile, are provided to help you keep track of children's progress.

The Student Record Form for each test follows it in the Student Test Booklet. Class Profiles for all tests in this manual appear at the back of the manual. Another recording option is the Student Progress Card that is available separately. The Student Progress Card allows you to keep a cumulative record of an individual child's *Literature Works* test scores as he or she progresses through the various grade levels of the program.

Completing the Student Record Form

The Student Record Form is a convenient record of a child's test performance. The form groups test items by strand (i.e., Comprehension) and skill (i.e., Sequence). The form can show at a glance which skills a child understands and which skills may need reinforcement.

The following pointers will help you complete the Student Record Form:

1. Score the test by comparing the child's answers with those on the Answer Key.

2. For every CORRECT answer, place a mark on the line next to the item number on the Student Record Form.

3. Write the number of correct answers in the column labeled Student Skill Score.

4. Add the number correct within a strand to get the Student Strand Score and write the number in the column labeled Student Strand Score.

5. Add up the strand scores to get the Total Test Score and write it in the appropriate space.

Using the Class Profile

The Class Profile is designed to help you plan appropriate activities for children either individually or in groups. Use the Class Profile to record Skills Assessment scores, to identify specific skills for which a child or group of children may need help, and to record sources for additional instruction and practice.

The Skills Assessments are designed to help you determine how well a child understands each tested skill taught in one or more themes. If a child scores 80 percent or higher in a skill area, he or she probably has a good understanding of the skill. A child whose score is low may benefit from extra help before going on to the next theme.

The Suggested Passing Score of 80 percent is only a guideline; use your own good judgment to decide if that score is an appropriate indication of how well children are doing.

To help you determine if a child has answered 80 percent of the questions correctly, the Suggested Passing Scores for each skill, strand, and the complete test are shown in the column labeled "Suggested Passing Score" on the Student Record Form. These scores are shown as ratios. For example, the Suggested Passing Score for Vocabulary is 8/10 or 80 percent. (The Suggested Passing Score also appears on the Skills Assessment Class Profile.)

An important part of interpreting test scores is relating test results to the individual child. Before assigning extra help to children scoring below 80 percent on a skill, you may want to go over specific test items with them individually to find out why they chose the answers that they did. You may discover, for example, that a child did not fully understand the directions but has, in fact, a good understanding of the skill. In that case, you may decide that additional practice is not needed, and you may wish to adjust the child's score.

If a child does need more help, you will find the program components containing materials for additional practice and reinforcement listed at the bottom of the Class Profile. You may wish to identify, list, and assign additional practice using pages from the Practice Books or reteaching masters from the SourceBank.

Item	Answer	Skill	Item	Answer	Skill
1.	B	tested vocabulary	16.	C	reality and fantasy
2.	C	tested vocabulary	17.	B	compare and contrast
3.	A	tested vocabulary	18.	B	reality and fantasy
4.	A	tested vocabulary	19.	C	phonograms
5.	C	tested vocabulary	20.	A	phonograms
6.	A	tested vocabulary	21.	C	phonograms
7.	B	tested vocabulary	22.	B	phonograms
8.	A	tested vocabulary	23.	A	consonant blends
9.	C	tested vocabulary	24.	B	consonant blends
10.	B	tested vocabulary	25.	C	consonant blends
11.	B	reality and fantasy	26.	A	consonant blends
12.	C	compare and contrast	27.	B	abc order
13.	B	reality and fantasy	28.	A	abc order
14.	A	compare and contrast	29.	B	abc order
15.	C	compare and contrast	30.	C	abc order

Teacher's Guide skill lessons for Theme 5 provide instructional support and suggest materials.

Grade _____ Test Date _____

Names* STRAND Skill	VOCAB-ULARY tested vocabulary	COMPREHENSION		PHONICS	
		compare & contrast	reality & fantasy	phono-grams	consonant blends
Suggested Passing Scores: ▶	8/10	3/4	3/4	3/4	3/4
1					
2					
3					
4					
5					
6					
7					
8					
9					
10					
11					
12					
13					
14					
15					
16					
17					
18					
19					
20					
21					
22					
23					
24					
25					
Number of Students Below Suggested Passing Score					
Practice Book (page numbers)					
SourceBank					

* Enter students' raw scores for each Skill; circle all scores that meet or exceed the Suggested Passing Score.

Teacher _____ School Name _____

STUDY
SKILLS

abc
order

3/4   Recommendations _____

_____   _____

_____   _____

_____   _____

_____   _____

_____   _____

_____   _____

_____   _____

_____   _____

_____   _____

_____   _____

_____   _____

_____   _____

_____   _____

_____   _____

_____   _____

_____   _____

_____   _____

_____   _____

_____   _____

_____   _____

_____   _____

_____   _____

Item	Answer	Skill	Item	Answer	Skill
1.	A	tested vocabulary	16.	B	drawing conclusions
2.	A	tested vocabulary	17.	C	drawing conclusions
3.	C	tested vocabulary	18.	A	cause and effect
4.	B	tested vocabulary	19.	A	short vowels
5.	C	tested vocabulary	20.	B	short vowels
6.	A	tested vocabulary	21.	B	short vowels
7.	B	tested vocabulary	22.	C	short vowels
8.	B	tested vocabulary	23.	A	long vowels
9.	C	tested vocabulary	24.	B	long vowels
10.	C	tested vocabulary	25.	C	long vowels
11.	B	cause and effect	26.	A	long vowels
12.	A	drawing conclusions	27.	B	digraphs
13.	C	cause and effect	28.	C	digraphs
14.	C	drawing conclusions	29.	A	digraphs
15.	B	cause and effect	30.	C	digraphs

Teacher's Guide skill lessons for Theme 6 provide instructional support and suggest materials.

Grade _____ Test Date _____

	STRAND	VOCAB-ULARY	COMPREHENSION		PHONICS	
	Skill	tested vocabulary	cause & effect	draw conclusions	digraphs	short vowels
Names*	Suggested Passing Scores: ▶	8/10	3/4	3/4	3/4	3/4
1						
2						
3						
4						
5						
6						
7						
8						
9						
10						
11						
12						
13						
14						
15						
16						
17						
18						
19						
20						
21						
22						
23						
24						
25						
Number of Students Below Suggested Passing Score						
Practice Book (page numbers)						
SourceBank						

* Enter students' raw scores for each Skill; circle all scores that meet or exceed the Suggested Passing Score.

long
vowels
3/4   Recommendations _____

_____   _____

_____   _____

_____   _____

_____   _____

_____   _____

_____   _____

_____   _____

_____   _____

_____   _____

_____   _____

_____   _____

_____   _____

_____   _____

_____   _____

_____   _____

_____   _____

_____   _____

_____   _____

_____   _____

_____   _____

_____   _____

ACKNOWLEDGMENTS

COVER: *Design:* Dinardo Design; *Illustration:* Ashley Van Etten.